Micro Poetry

A Moment for the Soul

Kenzo Amariyo

Copyright © 2023 Kenzo Amariyo

All rights reserved.

No part of this publication may be reproduced, distributed, or transmitted in any forms or by any means, including photocopying, recording, or any electronic or mechanical methods, without the prior written permission of the named publisher or author. Exceptions are in the case of brief quotations embodied in reviews and certain other noncommercial uses permitted by copyright law.

1st Print 2021

2nd Print 2023

Tenshi Publishing

Seaton, Devon UK

Contact: bookpublisher@tenshipublishing.com

Paperback: ISBN-13: 978-1-7399170-2-9
E-Book: ISBN-13: 978-1-7399170-3-6

Cover Designed by **'GetCovers'**

Contents

Book One 1

    Take Heart 3

    What Happens If? 4

    Enter Into Solitude 5

    Wander the Desert 6

    Life 7

    Self-Love 8

    Forgive Yourself 9

    Heal and Dance 10

    Share Your Pain 11

    Bleed Your Heart 12

    A True Master 13

    Choose Wisely 14

    Mind What You Serve 15

    Be Not Afraid 16

- Fulfil Your Soul 17
- The Cycle of Life 18
- Silence 19
- The River of Life 20
- Trials 21
- As the Mist Settles 22
- The Light Shines 23
- Loss 24
- Remember 25
- Entry Points 26
- Teach the Children 27
- Healing 28
- Time 29
- Floating Through Space 30
- She Pulls Me 31
- Emotional Intelligence 32
- Meet Me 33
- Same Direction – Different Track 34
- Change 35

Conquer the Evil Within 36

Enter the Sanctuary 37

Be a Good Leader 38

The Best Thing to Hold onto in Life 39

Create that Which We Want in Love 40

The Sun Sets on All 41

Holding the Space 42

Rest Awhile 43

Turmoil Strikes the Heart of the People ... 44

Gardeners of Our Mind 45

Two Ways – Two Outcomes 46

Be Brave Enough 47

Sometimes 48

Spirit Shines on Me 49

Protect Your Awakening 50

Fear and Courage 51

In the Stillness 52

Silence Is 53

Following Life 54

- Radiate Nectar 55
- Speak it into Existence 56
- That Secret Place 57
- Dream It 58
- Student or Master 59
- The Jewels of Our Heart 60
- Who Is Family? 61
- Follow the Right Religion 62
- Practice, Practice, Practice 63
- Intelligent but Not Always Loving 64
- Make Each Moment Count 65
- An Island 66
- Gratitude for Life 67
- Acceptance and Diversity 68
- Go Within 69
- Unconditional Love 70
- Depths without Measure 71
- Embrace Life – Live Your Potential 72
- Listen to Nature 73

When I See	74
Part of the Whole	75
Scourged	76
The Puzzle called Life	77
Rabbits in Burrows	78
Attachment Brings Loss	79
The Pains of Loss	80
Non-Attachment	81
Death – A Continuation of Life	82
Intimacy with God	83
Universal Knowledge	84
Self-Reflection	85
Find Happiness in Life	86
Be As Owl	87
Know Your Roots	88
Reach Out in Love	89
Desire Reconciliation	90
Re-Write Your Story	91
Heal the Past	92

- Beyond Today 93
- Clarity of Mind 94
- The Wind Blows... 95
- Time for Me 96
- Educate Yourself.. 97
- Step into Awareness 98
- The Search.. 99
- Stripped but Not of Attitude 100

Book Two 101
- The Chaotic Life 103
- Our Sole Purpose 104
- Unconditional Love 105
- Tortured Minds... 106
- A New Day 107
- Look to the Light.. 108
- Broken Dreams 109
- The Road to Self-Healing.......................... 110
- Giving.. 111
- Death to Self 112

No King Here	113
A Servant	114
A Lighthouse	115
Cherry Blossoms	116
Mother's Day	117
Loss on Mother's Day	118
Beating Wings	119
Nature Speaks	120
Wisdom	121
Slowly	122
Be Mindful	123
Be Ready	124
An Endless Ocean	125
Blessed Are We	126
Blue Skies	127
Feathered Friends	128
Floating	129
Paving a Way	130
The Creative Seed	131

Rise Up	132
Ask Oneself	133
Dreaming Dog	134
Know Yourself	135
To Forgive	136
Turn Your Cheek	137
The Final Straw	138
Rainwater	139
Disabled Not Ill	140
Our Stories	141
Make the Most of Opportunities	142
Love and Be Love	143
Clackety, Clack, Clack	144
The Fruit of Labour	145
If	146
Worth More than Gold	147
It's Here	148
The Clock Keeps Ticking	149
Be Love	150

I Hope	151
My Reflection	152
How I Start My Day	153
Be Not Ashamed	154
Songs of the Night	155
Reflection	156
Untamed Thoughts	157
The Lost Soul	158
Shhhh	159
My Soul Hears	160
A Wall Made of Tears	161
Pure Love	162
Feel Her	163
Horse Woman	164
Full Bodied Words	165
Waiting for the Clock	166
Water Your Soul	167
Unspoken Words	168
Open the Door	169

For Me, Life Is 170

My Glass 171

Love 172

Life 173

Sexual Abuse 174

Serenity 175

Gentle Footsteps 176

Remember the Feelings 177

Let Love In... 178

It's A New Day... 179

Blown Glass.. 180

We Always Want.. 181

Look Deeper... 182

Make Today Count.................................... 183

I Remember 184

Angels Lamenting...................................... 185

Silver Lining 186

The Fool.. 187

The Dance of Spirit 188

The Inner Mill Pond	189
Through the Eyes of Love	190
The Vessel	191
A Paradox of Life	192
Tears Fall	193
Silk Scarves	194
The Work of a Poet	195
How Deep We Are	196
Be Open – Be Held	197
Be More Attentive	198
Trust	199
Emotional Freedom	200
Book Three	**201**
Submerged	203
Till the Ground	204
Expand Your View	205
Be Gentle	206
The Breath of Life	207
Reflections	208

Discover..209

Nature Holds Me..........................210

Rainbow People............................211

The Divine Within 212

Be That Poppy...............................213

Natures Touch 214

Time to Let Go..............................215

Whole 216

No-One's Home............................217

Remember......................................218

Too Much News 219

Love Is All We Have...................220

New Life 221

Live or Die.....................................222

Droplets of Rain...........................223

Yearning Souls 224

If I Touched Your Soul...............225

The Winds of Change................226

Listen...227

In His Arms 228

Follow Your Path 229

Self-Discipline Brings Pleasure 230

Floating 231

The Gift of Silence 232

Waking Up 233

Breathe Life 234

United We Stand 235

Stand Strong 236

Healing from Loss 237

Deep Loss 238

Gratitude 239

Teatime 240

Be Present 241

Born to Fly 242

Be Open 243

Be Cleansed 244

Drink Spiritual Waters 245

Health Guidelines 246

- Lessons Learnt 247
- Held by the Vortex 248
- A Kiss of Death 249
- The Pendulum of Life 250
- Rain Fell 251
- Water Love 252
- Individual Drops 253
- Reaching Out 254
- A Multi-Cultural Heart 255
- When I Look 256
- One Heart, One Soul 257
- Blossoms and Smiles 258
- A Smile 259
- Without Words 260
- Sing Your Song 261
- Never Alone 262
- The Fog Lifts 263
- Be Propelled 264
- Be Refreshed 265

Find the Blessings 266
Angel of Death 267
Life Goes On 268
Time to Sleep 269
A Yarn to Be 270
Cradled In Peace 271
Be Love and Acceptance 272
Compassion 273
Be Kindness 274
True Happiness 275
Isolation – An Opportunity 276
Restrictions 277
Distraction 278
Into the Depths 279
Have No Regrets 280
The Problem 281
Deafening Silence 282
Perspectives 283
Island Style 284

Cleansing Winds	285
Caught In a Web	286
The Rainbow	287
People of the Rainbow	288
No Favourites	289
No Hierarchy in Oneness	290
We Are One	291
The Question to Ask	292
The Sun Shines	293
Waiting	294
The Edges of My Mind	295
Bringing Wholeness	296
Gender Neutral – The Key to Equality	297
Be the Change You Want to See	298
True Power	299
I Sneeze	300
Stay Strong	301
Heaven and Hell	302
Book Four	303

Gone but Not Forgotten 305

Sing 306

Flowing 307

Silently 308

River of Compassion 309

Success is In the Climb 310

Perceptions 311

New Buds 312

Green Fingers 313

I Just Know 314

Listen to the Call 315

Connect Daily 316

Slay that Giant 317

Clouds Hang Low 318

Stand Tall 319

Accepting Now 320

Experiences 321

Reflections 322

Words 323

- Love 324
- Reality 325
- Wake Up, Wake Up Everyone 326
- Count Your Blessings 327
- Sadness 328
- Inner Peace 329
- Success 330
- Spiritual Enlightenment 331
- Softly, Softly 332
- Silence Within 333
- What Is Life? 334
- The Curtains are Drawn 335
- Find Your Centre 336
- Riches 337
- Catalyst for Change 338
- Mindfulness 339
- Silence 340
- Sunset 341
- Functional Neurological Disorder 342

Dementia 343

The Pains of Dementia 344

How Beautiful Life Is 345

Sparkling Dew...346

Every Time 348

Toxic Relationships 349

Prepare..350

Your Smile Shines.....................................352

Micro Poetry

Book One

Kenzo Amariyo

Take Heart

The rain falls gently
Like the tears of angels
Weeping for the lost souls of past.

The flowers bow their heads
Bearing the weight of those tears
Wondering how long it will last.

But like all things
Tears come and go
And never does a sad day stay.

So, if your day
Is filled with tears
Take heart, it will soon go away.

What Happens If?

The world keeps moving, spinning around
We're oft' unaware as it makes no sound
Earth revolves despite how we feel
It holds us safe, quite surreal.

We take it for granted each and every day
Never stopping to think: *"What made it this way?"*
We naturally look down if something drops
But what happens if the earth stops?

Enter Into Solitude

If we are brave enough to enter solitude
We silence our mouths, not our heart
We silence the flurry of thoughts
Whilst listening intently
To the river of life
As it flows freely
Into our being
Enveloping
Our soul
In love.

Wander the Desert

Wander the desert of your heart
For within solitude, we find much wisdom
And from such wisdom
Fruit will grow
Watered by the soul's spring.

Life

Life…………. what is it?
If it isn't our own canvas
With which we create
Our own masterpiece.

Self-Love

Love thyself deeply
So that in those quiet moments
You can feel strong like the oak
Empowered from the roots.

Forgive Yourself

Forgive yourself
That you too may feel loved
By the one person who knows your heart
YOU!

Heal and Dance

Her tears fell
Like a gentle beat of a drum
But upon awakening
She was able to dance to her own rhythm.

Share Your Pain

Your pain and suffering
Is not meant to be hidden beneath shame and guilt.

It is meant to be shared
That others can grow and learn how to heal.

Bleed Your Heart

Let your heart bleed like a river running over white sand.

So that as it dries
What was bound is set free
So that others may learn and be blessed.

A True Master

A true Master
Master's himself
And becomes a servant to those in need.

Choose Wisely

We all have the same choice
To be a slave to our physical passions
Or the master of them.

Mind What You Serve

Do not boast about your spiritual practice.
Boasting is like serving the hungry an empty bowl.

Share with humility, love and compassion
Then all will be fed.

Be Not Afraid

Be not afraid of what others may do to you
Be afraid of what you constantly do to yourself
We are often our own worst enemy.

Fulfil Your Soul

Let thy soul
Fulfil its deepest desire
To be righteous and heavenly
So that its self-made music of love
Would be heard by all who have ears to hear.

The Cycle of Life

The waves gently lap against the sand
The sun is setting on another day
Much has been accomplished.

Each day, I move closer to a goal
That I never reach
For at every milestone
The light shines further.

Silence

Silence fills my soul
Peace washes over me
Like gentle rain over the trees
Bringing a new awakening.

The River of Life

I quietly observe the constant changes of what is and was
The river of life washes over all things
Reshaping, smoothing, moulding.

I flow willingly with my dear friend –
Change
And I am eternally blessed to see a greater version
Of that which I had already built.

Trials

Trials come and go
How difficult they are is dependant
Upon our attitude towards them.

As the Mist Settles

As the mist settles
It hides what was,
Bringing attention
To what is now in focus
A new day begins.

The Light Shines

The light shines brightly
The long tunnel now seems short
Much has dropped away.

Loss

Time was not enough
Your sun was setting so fast
Our future now gone
I watched and waited until
You drifted gently away.

Remember

I look in your eyes
And I see a reflection
Of the love you have
For all of humanity.

I remember who I am.

Entry Points

Our birth and our death
Are beautiful entry points
Into time and space
We don't remember our birth
And we need not fear our death.

Teach the Children

Teach the children love
Teach them to love all beings
Then they will know
That all beings are worth their life
And are deserving of love.

Healing

The stars shone brightly
No-one knew her inner pain
She sat quietly
And let the moon's energy
Fill her to overflowing.

Time

Time……. It is so precious.
It comes and goes without a thought
It doesn't process its existence
It just travels, continually.

Giving opportunities for us all
To create that which we desire
It is the healer of many pains
And the bringer of many suns.

Floating Through Space

Distance
Space and time
Thoughts come and go
No need to hold onto anything
Floating through space
Consciousness
Pure clarity
Light.

She Pulls Me

Full
Like the moon
Feeling her pull at night
No sleep – but a deep connection.

Emotional Intelligence

When we know and understand the
emotions that we are experiencing

And when we have learnt how to manage
those same emotions

We then become conscious of the affect
they can have on those around us.

Emotional Intelligence – Know Thyself

Meet Me

Meet me in the depth of the forest
Where silence weaves itself into my being.

Where the only sounds are of the birds
And the crack of old dry branches beneath my feet.

Where I listen to nature's stories
And where every sound is like a flute
playing a song of love in my heart.

Meet me there – so that in the silence of time
Our souls may sing as one.

Same Direction – Different Track

I don't follow the crowd
I follow my intuition
We may walk in the same direction
But often I will be on a different track.

Although I walk alone
I am not lonely
And if I am in your life
It is for a reason
And for a time.

Change

You do not change people by taking away their freedom.

You change people by being such an inspirational example that they cannot help but desire to be as you.

Change does not always happen in this lifetime.

Conquer the Evil Within

When we conquer the evil within
We improve collective consciousness

We all have a responsibility
To be the best we can.

Do not let the opportunity slip by.

Enter the Sanctuary

We have to grow from the inside out
Go within and find your spiritual guide.

Teachers offer examples of correct living
By copying them, we learn a way of being.

But that may not be the correct way for all
Listen, hear, and follow your inner guide.

Enter the sanctuary.

Be a Good Leader

Learn to be a good leader
Leadership isn't just about employees
Leadership is also about leading yourself
Leading others by your actions
By the way you live your life.

A good leader leads by example
And paves a way for others to follow –
If they choose to.

The Sun Sets on All

Sadness in their hearts
Death – on so many levels
The sun sets on all.

Holding the Space

I remain detached from the chaos of life
Not because I do not care
But because we need calming influential energies
In order to re-establish peace.

Rest Awhile

Don't go to bed with angry thoughts
With hatred burning like a torch.

Let all pain slip away for now
Breathe in deep, relax the brow.

For restful sleep cannot take place
Whilst anger rests upon your face.

Turmoil Strikes the Heart of the People

Fighting, screaming
Shouting hate
Protesting for rights
From morn till late.

Chaos burning
In people's hearts
Wanting revenge
For lives ripped apart.

But sooner or later
Justice will be done
And peace will reside
In everyone.

Gardeners of Our Mind

Our mind is our garden
We plant what we choose
Some of us win
Others lose.

If you want a sweet apple tree
Don't plant a lemon
Weed out your mind
If you're aiming for Heaven.

Two Ways – Two Outcomes

Scattered mind
Erratic life
Chaos.

Collected mind
Grounded life
Peace.

Be Brave Enough

It is common knowledge
When one door closes another will open.

The issue is whether we are brave enough
To walk through that open door!

Sometimes

Sometimes......
You just have to take a step back
Re-assess.......
And make changes in order to move forward.

Spirit Shines on Me

Today my need is silence, stillness, quiet thoughts
And all the beauty on offer that simply cannot be bought.

The beauty in the flowers the beauty in the trees
The beauty in life itself, which always aims to please.

So today I will be lost and revelling in my space
Where Spirit will shine its light, right across my face.

Protect Your Awakening

There will come a time
When things seem to have returned to normal
The temptation for many
Will be to go straight back to how it was before.

Covid-19 taught many a new way of living
A new way of being
Protect that learning, that awakening
Like a lion protects her cubs.

Fear and Courage

We cannot stand with one foot in both camps for long
Sooner or later, we have to make a choice
Stay in the familiar
Or step out into uncharted ground.

Fear holds you back, courage carries you on.

In the Stillness

In the stillness of time
We become
All that we truly are.

We learn self-love
Self-acceptance, self-worth
And we discover our spiritual roots.

Like a caterpillar to a butterfly
We learn to die to self
So that we may live again.

Silence Is

Silence......
Is the precursor to hearing
Hearing is the precursor to doing
Doing is the precursor to transformation
Transformation into our full potential is
why we are here.

Following Life

Life………
It leads us along unknown paths
It urges us to tread on meadows and rough plains.

We tentatively follow its lead
Not sure of where it will take us
But trusting in experience
And in the knowledge that it always leads to blessings.

Radiate Nectar

If our heart is like nectar,
We will radiate sweetness into the world
And others will be drawn to us
Like a bee to the flower.

Speak it into Existence

The bible teaches us in Genesis
That the world was first envisioned
Felt and desired
Then spoken into existence.

We too must envision, feel, desire
And then speak out the world we desire
into existence.

That Secret Place

From that secret place of creation
Create the best version of you
Feed it, water it
And like a seed
It will grow into its full beauty and grace.

Dream It

Dream…………
And when you dream
Dream so big you can't imagine it
possible.

Then pick up your courage
And dive straight into the dreamy lake of
possibilities
Where dreams become your reality.

Student or Master

When we master the art of mindfulness
We no longer need to practice it
For it becomes our way of being.

The student practices
The master lives.

The Jewels of Our Heart

The jewels of our heart
Lay quietly awaiting
Their birth.

Feel them
Embrace them
Breathe life into them.

Who Is Family?

Your family may live with you
They may be scattered around the world
They may or may not be blood relatives.

Family – The people who accept you and support you.

Follow the Right Religion

It is not the religion that matters
What matters is whether it brings the best out of you
And whether it is built on a foundation of love, compassion and forgiveness for all.

Practice, Practice, Practice

Practice kindness
Practice peace
Practice love
Practice forgiveness.

Then you will experience the true wonders of life.

Intelligent but Not Always Loving

We are intelligent beings
But sometimes we are not loving beings
The most intelligent thing we could perhaps do
Would be to learn to love unconditionally.

Make Each Moment Count

In the presence of the Divine
I am reminded of my purpose
The very reason for my being
I am reminded of how short this life is.

I am reminded that at the blink of an eye
Any one of us could be called back home
So make each moment count
Let each moment reflect the goodness of your soul.

An Island

Today…… I remain an island
Distant and free
Boats are welcome to moor,
People are welcome to step ashore
But I remain in the stillness of my heart
Mindful of self and others
But still.

Let the silence of your heart renew your
mind and spirit.

Gratitude for Life

Life is a gift
That we must choose to receive
We must trust that it is good
We must truly believe.

Believe that as we unwrap
All the paper and the string
That only love and hope
It will surely bring.

And the more gratitude we show
Each and every day
For all that we receive
Will bring much more our way.

Acceptance and Diversity

When we see people as people
They will be people
When we see people through borders
They will be different people.

Acceptance and diversity
Are issues of the heart.

Go Within

If you want to find God
Go within.

If you want to lead a spiritual life
Go within.

If you want to drink spiritual waters
Go within.

You cannot reach the depth of your being
unless you go within.

Unconditional Love

Unconditional love
Given freely
No strings attached
Brings healing to many a broken soul.

Depths without Measure

We will never know the true depths
To which we can truly love.

Nor will we ever know the true heights
To which we can soar.

For once we reach what we thought was the end
We realise it was just the beginning.

Embrace Life – Live Your Potential

A new day starts
A new journey begins
Or perhaps the same journey continues
Up and over new horizons
Through new forests
Forests that offer new awareness
Renewed strength and fresh insight.

Embrace life and live to your full potential.

Listen to Nature

Life teaches us to grasp
To hold on
To claim as our own.

Nature teaches us to hold lightly
To let go
To relinquish ownership.

When I See

When I see *'parents'* I see through my child eyes
When I see *'people'* I see through my adult eyes
When I see *'opportunities to practice love'* I see through God's eyes.

Part of the Whole

When we remove labels from people
They become *just people*
Aspects of ourselves
Equal and lovable.
They become
Part of you
And part of me
And part of the whole
We become unified not separate.

Scourged

We hunt like scavengers
Looking for hope, love, acceptance
We do not feel them because
We do not love and accept ourselves.

We sometimes feel scourged
By life and circumstance
Not realising that it is often
Us that holds the whip.

Let go – And you shall live.

The Puzzle called Life

Life!
What is it if it isn't a puzzle?
Where we try to fit pieces together
To understand our existence and purpose
And hope that by the close of business
We manage to complete the puzzle
And discover that which we did not know
and searched for.

Rabbits in Burrows

The day is closing
The silence can now be heard
Rabbits in burrows.

Attachment Brings Loss

My experience in regard to the death and dying of loved ones is simply this:

If I cling to what I believe, understand, or know about life and death

Rather than clinging to the person concerned

Then a significant amount of loss is not experienced.

The greater the attachment to the person
The greater the sense of loss.

The Pains of Loss

We feel the pains of loss when our loved ones die because of our attachment to them.

This attachment is often where we source our identity from.

An Indian proverb says: *There is **No** death only a change of worlds.*

Non-Attachment

We are habitually attached
To our possessions in life
And not just things but husband and wife.

Life's hardest lesson
Is to start to let go
Non-attachment brings freedom – did you know?

Death – A Continuation of Life

I see death as a continuation of life
Rather than another life.

Like caterpillar to butterfly
We merely abandon the body and
continue to fly.

If we see both life and perceived death as
one journey
Then we are only separated through the
physical veil of existence.

Intimacy with God

As you evolve spiritually
The Divine Source
May not appear to be any closer to your grasp
But your connection with it
Will eventually feel
More intimate and personal.

Universal Knowledge

Universal mind contains all knowledge
And as we are all aspects of that same mind
We all have the potential
To gain so much more knowledge
Than what we perceive to be possible.

Self-Reflection

The universe exists, that we may see the reflection of its creator.
We exist so that we may learn to *be* as our true reflection – the universe.

Find Happiness in Life

I know what it's like
Living in a country that's poor,
Where there isn't enough food
And not even a door.

Where many use sheets
To keep off the sun,
And cardboard for a bed
Wake up everyone!

But when you look past the poverty
There are still many smiles,
Their appreciation for life
Stretches for miles.

Find happiness in life.

Be As Owl

The owl sits and hoots
Alone but not alone
Watching, waiting
Aware of his surroundings
But silent in heart
And enveloped in stillness.

Know Your Roots

I live in the knowing
That there is something
So much greater than I
Which supports me
And which I am part of.

Know your roots.

Reach Out in Love

If you are going to reach out to someone
Ensure you are reaching out in love
Check your motives.

Reach out in sincerity
Not for your own profit or gain.

Desire Reconciliation

To sit and ponder on the hurt of the past
Without the desire for reconciliation
Can be like re-opening a wound.

Re-Write Your Story

We have the power to re-write our story.

We may not be able to re-write events.

But we can re-write how we look at it.

And how it informs our future.

Heal the Past

Your past does not have to remain the horror story of your life.

It can be the healing story that sets you free and informs your future.

Beyond Today

Think beyond your problems
Think beyond your pain
Tomorrow the sun may shine
It won't always look like rain.

Don't give up on hope
Don't let go of dreams
Soon there will be laughter
It won't always be inner screams.

Look beyond today – create a different tomorrow.

Clarity of Mind

If we want clarity within our mind
We must look within our heart
We must seek solitude
And heal the broken part.

We must awaken to our true self
Knowing we are part of our Divine
Then we will start to sense
That clarity of mind.

The Wind Blows

The winds of change
Sweep over and through
Blowing away the old
Bringing in the new.

No point holding on
No point fighting change
Everything I need
Will surely remain.

Time for Me

I've been up for several hours now
I've even walked the dog
The sun was shining brightly
No wind, no rain, no fog.

I've even done some Twittering
So now it's time for me
So, I am off to get myself
A nice cuppa tea!

Educate Yourself

The only truly educated person
Is the one who knows how to evolve
Into a better and spiritual expression
Of whom they currently are.

Step into Awareness

It would seem that no one is exempt from the less desirable experiences through life.

In which case......

The best way forward is to make each experience a stepping stone to greater awareness.

The Search

When we fulfil our spiritual desires
The irritants of life drop away
Like sand from the open hand.

Our search for meaning
Is a deep inner search
It always has been.

Stripped but Not of Attitude

My journey alongside a disability
Has stripped me of many freedoms.

But it hasn't taken away my choice
For which attitude I will hold each day.

How we interpret life
Is often built upon the attitude we choose
to take.

Micro Poetry

Book Two

Kenzo Amariyo

The Chaotic Life

You cannot live a chaotic life
And expect to feel at peace
He who lives in chaos
Lives without peace.

Our Sole Purpose

If the sole purpose of our being
Is to kindle a light,
In the darkness of our existence
Have we fulfilled that purpose?

Unconditional Love

We need to hold another's heart
Gently in our palms
We need to wrap it up in love
And cradle it in our arms
We need to treat it with respect
Show unconditional love
And then the angels will rejoice
With tears from up above.

Tortured Minds

So many people
Living with broken hearts
Tortured minds
Emotions spilt endlessly
On a floor of broken dreams and trust.

A New Day

The sun breaks open
A new day for everyone
Life – Another shot.

Look to the Light

The moon shone brightly
Bringing light into a dark world
The stars stood by
Confirming the light
Reminding us that,
No matter what happens
We need to look to the light.

Broken Dreams

The world is full of broken dreams
Broken hearts that shout their screams
The world is full of suffering and pain
People hurting others again and again.

But despite the bad we can see
I do believe both you and me
Are on this earth to shine a light
To make things better
And make life bright.

The Road to Self-Healing

Travelling down a rose
Passing long sharp thorns
Heading for the roots
Where lies all things forlorn.

I'm searching for the cause
Of all my suffering and pain
I'm looking to bring healing
To myself through tears like rain.

And once I have achieved
All that needs to be done
I will travel back up the rose
Where I can feel at one.

Giving

Another client
Another body
Needing more than what I give.

Petrissage, kneading,
Some hope
That they may live.

Another hour
Another day
The difference – will I be?

20 odd years a therapist
Now who will massage me?

Death to Self

Humbleness, the best pie you could eat
Servanthood, the highest mountain you could climb
Spiritual waters, the best wine you could drink.
Death to self, the quickest way to life.

No King Here

Wealth didn't make him rich.
It was choosing to be a servant to others,
Not a king.
That's what made him rich.

A Servant

Freedom comes from abandoning our will
For the greater will of the universe
We come that we may serve.

A Lighthouse

I stand as a lighthouse
For the weary of heart
For those who are down cast
Shipwrecked – torn apart.

I stand strong and silent
As I light up the way
Making the night
More like the day.

I avert you from danger
In the darkest of night
But you must desire
To see the light.

Cherry Blossoms

Cherry blossoms
Pour forth from your lips
As they fall, they sound as angel's voices
I am momentarily enthroned by your love.

I am captivated by all that you are
And all that you are to me
I willingly drown in your loving words
That I may live for eternity in your heaven.

Mother's Day

Mother you are an angel
An angel without wings
You are always there to give a hug
And help with many things.

Today for some it's special
But you are special every day
Just because you are
The best in every way.

Loss on Mother's Day

I write this poem for all the mums
Who have lost a little one
It may be *'Mother's Day'* for some
But for others, your babe has gone.

But mothers you still are my dears
And your tears I wipe away
And remind you forever more
You will meet again one day.

Beating Wings

Refrain from flapping your tongue,
And hear the beating wings of your heart.

Nature Speaks

Nature speaks
That we may listen
And learn to hold our tongue.

Wisdom

And mind said to heart:
"Why don't you listen to me?"

And heart replied:
"Wisdom comes with two evenly balanced wings, without me, you are a one winged bird"

Slowly

Slowly
The mind unfolds
The unconscious becomes conscious
And what once was
Now drops away
As light brings new awareness.

Be Mindful

Be mindful of self
Be mindful of what you sow
Like a tree by the water
It will surely grow.

Be Ready

Grasp not at life
Less you miss your ride to freedom
Be ready always
For you know not the time or place.

An Endless Ocean

And what is eternity?
Other than an endless ocean
Where the horizon
Is never reached.

A continuation of spirit life
With and without
A physical body.

Blessed Are We

Blessed are we
With open hearts
With minds of love and peace
That we can rest in natures arms
Like babes wrapped in a fleece.

Blue Skies

Blue skies overhead
A ball of yellow hanging high
Wrapped in warmth from natures hold
Relaxing…I give a sigh.

Feathered Friends

Tweeting private love songs
As light pushes back the dark
I don't understand their tweets
But on my heart, they leave a mark.

They leave a fresh reminder
Of the gifts that nature brings
Every single morning
When I listen to birds sing.

Floating

Floating…
On a lotus flower
Held safe by its roots
The sun warms my soul
A balmy summer day ahead.

Memories
Floating slowly by
Remind me that life is
Always a gift we are given
And one not to take for granted.

Paving a Way

Lots of work
That needs to be done
One step at a time
One by one.

Then each little step
Or each little stone
Will build a mountain
Where others can roam.

The Creative Seed

Creativity is a gift
That we have all been given
Take notice of it
And where you're surely driven.

The seeds are deeply planted
In rich and fertile ground
Just give it a little water
Then wait, just stick around.

And sooner than you think
You will feel those seeds start to grow
And will stay with you forever
Wherever you do go.

Rise Up

Fall into your self
Discover your potential
And rise to meet it.

Ask Oneself

One must ask themselves
Is it better to be loved
Or to be love?

Dreaming Dog

The dog now sleeping
Dreaming of his early walk
Tail wags
Momentary peace pervades.

Know Yourself

Know your true self well
Then you will be congruent
In all your actions.

To Forgive

To forgive others
Is to set two people free
You and the other.

Turn Your Cheek

When someone slaps you
Turn your cheek
Hold not a grudge
Be not weak.

The struggle is not
Yours to win
It is their pain
From deep within.

Resist the urge
To fight and hate
It is love that gets you
Through Heaven's gate.

The Final Straw

Her pain was a bloodshed story
With broken trust
And scenes that were gory
Forced to fight
For her life and her child
She fought as a lioness
Fierce not mild.

In the mist of rage
A tumultuous storm
She lost herself and whilst forlorn
Grabbed a knife
Fell onto him
Never again
Would her light be dimmed.

Rainwater

The sun is high
The warmth feels sweet
Way up high
My eyes did meet
A beautiful rainbow
Made just for me
Rainwater like tears
Fell from a tree
It hit my neck
And ran down my spine
I quivered – nature
This moment's all mine.

Disabled Not Ill

Disabled people
Are not always sickly
Some are happy
Some are prickly.

Some have health issues
Some do not
Many make the most
Of the health they have got.

So please don't assume
As I use a wheelchair
That my health is not good
That's unjust and not fair.

Our Stories

Sometimes our stories
Cut to the core
Reflecting our suffering
And those from before.

But our stories are important
And need to be shared
Then you will see
All those that cared.

Make the Most of Opportunities

Rubbish to one
A blessing to others
The rag-picker picking
Up clothes from two brothers.

She knows their value
She knows their worth
Working fingers to bone
Each day a new birth.

Love and Be Love

Love and be love – The whole universe rests on love.

Clackety, Clack, Clack

A neurological disorder
Prevents me from walking
But I can still reach out
It doesn't stop me talking.

But a hermit I am
And for that I am glad
I talk through my keyboard
Clackety, clack, clack.

The Fruit of Labour

Success isn't in the publishing of a book
It is in the self-belief that you can and do write the book.

Publishing the book
Is simply the fruit of your labour.

If

If I could give you one gift
It would be the ability
To see your full potential.

Worth More than Gold

Prisoner at the window
The weather has me tight
It really can get too much
Indoors from dawn till night.

I can't drive a car now
My wheelchair can't go fast
These are the times
I miss my freedom from the past.

I would throw on mac and boots
And be off right up the road
So be thankful for mobility
It's worth much more than gold.

It's Here

Snow falling
The wind howls
Like a wolf calling
Under a silver moon.

The Clock Keeps Ticking

How time fly's by....
The future becomes the present
The present becomes the past
Life – moving in fast motion
It seems to move so fast.

Birth – Life – Death…
It comes
And of that we have no say
Use your time wisely
Make it count every day.

Be Love

It was in mid-December
Leaves had all let go
I took my dog a walking
Walking in the snow.

Birds were singing sweetly
Such a joy to hear
It felt as if Heaven
Was singing in my ear.

I paused to listen intently
I didn't want to miss a note
On my heart that morning
"Be Love" was surely wrote.

I Hope

I hope my poems are meaningful
I hope they bring much light
I hope they are the difference
That makes a dark day bright.

I hope my words are whispers
That float down from above
Leaving kisses of compassion
To start your day with love.

My Reflection

Against the backdrop
Of the night
I feel and see my light.

How I Start My Day

My morning starts when the silence
Of the night is still in bloom
When all around is sleeping
Wrapped up in their cocoon.

When night songs are sung sweetly
Feeding my spirit and my soul
That's how I start my day
For it makes me feel so whole.

Be Not Ashamed

Be not ashamed
Of your weakness
Only the weak
Can be made strong.

Songs of the Night

Songs of the night
Are the echoes
Of my soul.

Reflection

Reflective mood – quiet whispers.

Untamed Thoughts

Thoughts…
Left untamed
Can become
The wolves
Of your
Consciousness.

The Lost Soul

He visited
Every night
He came through the wall
That adjoined
Both rooms.

Dark
Sullen
I hid beneath my sheet
Heart beating
A small child.

He looked
And went
Always into the wardrobe
In the morning
I looked – he was gone.

Shhhh

Silence – Rests upon my soul.

My Soul Hears

At the top
Of the mountain
I sit
In silence
Under the watchful eye
Of the moon
Whilst my soul
Connects to the stars
Their words
Unfathomable
Their meaning
Only comprehended
By my soul.

A Wall Made of Tears

She knew not
Of what true love was
Her childhood tears
Had become the wall
That kept love out.

Pure Love

Even my bones
Dissolve into
Your arms.
Your love
Melts
My
Soul.

Feel Her

The earth held her
Like a mother holds her newborn child
Lovingly, passionately
As if nothing else exists.

She felt the rhythm
The heart beat
Of our dear mother earth.

Horse Woman

And there she goes
With the wind in her hair
Running free
And wild.
She knows her power
Her strength
She knows how
To embrace
The earth
Below her feet.

Full Bodied Words

When you speak
Your words
Are like
A glass
Of red wine
Full bodied
And meaningful.

They embrace
And enliven
Every
Bud
Nestled
Within the
Cave of experience.

Waiting for the Clock

Darkness…. it's 5am.
Waiting….
For the turning of the clock.

Water Your Soul

Silence to the soul
Is like water
To the flower.

Unspoken Words

The dog sits
And stares
Intently
Piercing his victim - Me
To the soul.

It's time to walk the dog.

Open the Door

I opened the door
Love flowed out
Like a river
Flowing freely.

Be open to love.

For Me, Life Is

For me…
Life is not about
What I cannot do
But about
What I can do.

My Glass

On a good day
My glass is half full
On a better day
My glass is full.

There are no bad days
Only days with more
Opportunities to grow.

Love

Love….
Like a gentle flowing river
Singing its own song
Washing over and
Moving around obstacles
To keep the flow flowing.

Life

Life……
Filled with unexpected twists and turns
Roads that lead to other roads,
Hills and valleys.

We can do nothing
But be open to an ever changing tapestry
Of life.

Sexual Abuse

Sexual Abuse……
It happens behind closed doors
We don't want to talk about it
We sweep it under the floor.

I haven't had the experience
But I've experienced its pain
I've counselled many others
Who live with constant rain.

We MUST learn to talk about it
Their stories MUST be told
They need to have the liberty
To speak out and be bold.

Serenity

Stillness
Peace
No thoughts
Emptiness.

Full of the void.

Gentle Footsteps

Gentle footsteps
Leave no trail
Crisp leaves
Give way to the weight of your body.

Enchanted forest
Full of wisdom
Whispers fall
Like falling leaves within your soul.

Listen
Listen to its voice
Hear its longing to share wisdom
Listen – hear – give thanks – be blessed.

Remember the Feelings

When the weather is cold and dreary
Remember the feelings of spring
They are stored as *trigger words*
Held deep within.

Remember!

Winter outside
A warm spring day within.

Let Love In

They stood side by side
One rich, one poor
One dressed in emeralds
One rags to the floor.

I looked deep within
Was blinded by light
One reflected beauty
Such a grand sight.

The beauty was deep
It surpassed clothes and skin
The poor one was the rich one
For she'd let love right in.

It's A New Day

The sun shines through the window
And through my windows
It warms the earth
And my whole being
Peace settles upon the earth
And within my soul
It's a new day.

Blown Glass

We all unfold
As if we are in the hands
Of a master creator
A glass-smith.
Carefully being blown, crafted
Life being the torch that reshapes us
There are no mistakes
Only difference.

We Always Want

We always want the sunshine
We seldom want the rain
We want our lives filled
With happiness not pain.

Many try to hide
Their pain throughout their years
If we only understood
Life is smiles and also tears.

Our stories are our medicine
Our pain we need to face
Be brave, be courageous
Help the human race.

Look Deeper

Titles, labels
Wherever we go
They explain some things
But nobody knows
What truly lies
Within someone's heart
Take time to look
We know people in part.
Titles, labels
Don't define our soul
You have to look deeper
Than an earthly role.

Make Today Count

Silence fills the air
Peace is all around
The dawning of a new day.

Hold it tightly
For we never know
When our day will dawn.

Make today count.

I Remember

I remember him oh so well
As we stood face to face
His radiance
Would warm my heart
His presence
Would penetrate my very being
Love would just bubble up
From nowhere
He just had this incredible way
Of making everyday
A beautiful one.

Dear sun……how I miss you.

Angels Lamenting

The rain gently falls
Like tears from Angels
Lamenting the pains
Of our dear mother earth.

Silver Lining

From active to not
From outwards to inner
Can't do much housework
Can't often cook dinner.

Neurological issues
All reason to complain
And to be dragged down
With excruciating pain.

But the secret for me
Is the *'Silver Lining'*
I now have time
For writing and rhyming.

The Fool

The fool thinks
And thinks that nature
Has no voice.

Get up, get up
You fool
At 3am

And then tell me you can't
Hear and feel the deafening silent song
Of natures' sweet voice.

The Dance of Spirit

The breeze sleeps
All is resting
Relaxing.

The rain gently falls
Like tears dancing
As they land.

Cleansing all they touch
Cleansing, refreshing
Feeding
Just like
Spirit.

The Inner Mill Pond

The night is still
The whispers of 4.30am
Resonate with my spirit.

Peace lies still within
Like a mill pond
Alive but motionless.

Absorbing life from above
Ready to overflow
And feed that which needs feeding.

Through the Eyes of Love

When you look through your windows
And see less than beauty in someone
Pull down your shutters
And pause……

Remove judgement
Then look through your windows again.

The Vessel

Let your pen
Be the vessel
In which
Your heart pours.

A Paradox of Life

Death to one
Survival to another

A last breath for the deer
Another breath for the lion.

Tears Fall

Tears fall like rain
I catch them in the palms of my hand
Absorb them into my heart
They grow wings
And fly away.

Silk Scarves

Silk scarves so pure and soft
Makes even old look new
Then I remember the silkworms
Whilst in their safe cocoon
Are plunged into boiling water
To get their silk at ease
Silk scarves smell of death
I ask: *"Don't buy them, please"*

The Work of a Poet

The work of a poet is never done
The world is her pen
Hearts are her canvas.

How Deep We Are

Whilst the depth of the ocean
May reflect the depth of the unconscious mind.

The breadth of the earth reflects
The possibilities of the conscious mind.

Be Open – Be Held

The sky is blue, the sun radiates warmth
Out and down onto the lower spheres
Where all that takes note can hear
Its message of peace and love
And where all can feel
Its warmth as it
Gently holds
Us close.

Be More Attentive

If the depth of our life
Was seen as a reflection
Of our inner search for meaning
We would perhaps be more attentive.

Trust

When the path seems misty
And the way unclear
Focus your mind
Let go of fear.

Trust in the universe
And all that it knows
Trust that it will show you
The way you must go.

Emotional Freedom

The road to emotional freedom
Lies in the mind
Manage your mind
And you will manage your emotions.

Micro Poetry

Book Three

Kenzo Amariyo

Submerged

We are like fish….
Fully submerged in the very life force
That keeps us animated
And living
And half the time
We don't even realise the ocean in which we live.

Till the Ground

Prepare yourself
On all levels
So that you are ready
To receive
All that life has for you.

Expand Your View

Don't let your past
Limit your view of life
You are greater
Than what has happened to you.

Be Gentle

Be gentle as a feather
Floating on a summer breeze
So that you leave no footprints
On the hearts of those you meet.

The Breath of Life

Spread your wings
And let the breath of life
Be the wind that carries you forth
Into the next stage of your life.

Reflections

When they tell you
You are not good enough
Show empathy
And remember
They probably think that
About themselves.

We often act as mirrors
Reflecting the good
And the less good in others.

Discover

Touch the centre
Of your soul
That you may discover
All that you are
And all that you can be.

Nature Holds Me

Silence pours forth from my very being
Stillness fills my soul
The songs of sweet summer
Echo in my heart
Nature holds me
In the palm of its hand
That I may rest
And be refreshed.

Rainbow People

A new world of people evolved
The dark days were gone
The sun shone once again
Into the lives of those remaining
Gratitude was their new song
They lived as rainbow people.

The Divine Within

There is only one Divine Power in this universe
And we are all one within it and of it
And we all have use of it
Use it wisely.

Be That Poppy

Tall poppy syndrome
Threatens to hold you captive
Stand tall and be free.

Natures Touch

Sun caressed the earth
Rain watered the barrenness
Even the weak grew.

Time to Let Go

Trees bow with respect
To the coming forceful wind
It's time to let go.

Whole

Sun kisses our skin
Moon enters our emotions
Spirit breathes in life.

No-One's Home

They think she isn't thinking
As the eyes show no-one's home
Broken on the inside
Her spirit left to roam
Safer in the other world
Where most cannot be seen
She will never truly know
What could have truly been.

Remember

When life threatens to overwhelm
Step back.
Take the time to breathe
And let all pressures fall away.
Remember
You are not alone.

Too Much News

Too much news
Can drag you down
Take 10%
Of what makes you frown.

The other 90
Should make you smile
Then you will go
That extra mile.

You won't be so tired
Or completely drained
It will make you a pleasure
Instead of a pain.

Love Is All We Have

Love is all
We truly have.
Don't waste life
Holding onto resentments.

New Life

The sun shines on all
Bringing new life
New hope
And love.

Be open
And embrace your blessings
Life is for living.

Live or Die

The time came
Where she knew
It was time
It was now or never
Live or die.

Droplets of Rain

The tears fell
Like droplets of rain
Each one holding
Years of pain.

Death can bring
Much heartache and sorrow
But there are times
When it brings relief for tomorrow.

Yearning Souls

Broken souls
Litter the earth
Looking, yearning
For a fresh re-birth.

Where once again
They can travel through life
And find their peace
Leaving all strife.

If I Touched Your Soul

If I touched your soul
What would I find?
Love or hate
A heart that is kind?

If I touched your soul
How much pain would I feel?
Find what you need
To help yourself heal.

The Winds of Change

The winds of change
Sweep over the earth
For some it is joy and
Perhaps a new birth.

For others it is pain
Like a thorn in the flesh
Fighting, resisting
Tightly enmeshed.

Flow with the winds
Flow with the earth
Find the good
Find new self-worth.

Listen

Silence……
It opens doors
For your Spirit
To speak……
Listen.

In His Arms

Until that day….
Hold onto trust
And know
You have a place
Within the arms
Of Christ the Lord
Who will wipe
The tears from your face.

Follow Your Path

Be not afraid
To leave the *'norm'*
Be not afraid
To stand the storm.

We are all different
Like grains of sand
Don't let society
Make demands.

Follow your spirit
Honour your heart
Then from your true path
You will not depart.

Self-Discipline Brings Pleasure

Spirits entwine
Like whirls of energy
Separating and coming together
Like the ocean and the sand.

Self-discipline
Of the carnal nature
Brings new pleasures
You enter a new and richer land.

Floating

Currently floating
Through a conscious void
Thoughts just fleeting
Not a place to avoid
Slowly moving
Through time and space
Void of feelings
No need to race
Unconnected
From worries of the world
Me, the Universe
An energetic swirl.

The Gift of Silence

Feeling so much peace
Silence is my offering
Unable to speak.

Waking Up

It wasn't until
Death hung at the people's door
That they saw their blessings.

Breathe Life

Life is in the breath
Breathe in each moment deeply
Then you will know life.

United We Stand

Stand tall and be strong
We are not trees but forest
Together we stand.

Stand Strong

Nature comes and goes
The wheel of life keeps turning
We must be as the oak.

Healing from Loss

The virus took him
But it also took her heart
Then, healing rained down.

Deep Loss

His anger flourished
His panic flowed through his veins
Was she really gone?

Gratitude

Winter has now gone
Spring is here in her glory
Gratitude overflows.

Teatime

It's now 6:40
It's time to go
The birds are chirping
The mornings aglow
Chores to do
A spouse to hug
It's time for green tea
In a nice big mug.

Be Present

When you are present BE present
When you are away BE away

Be congruent to your needs
And the needs of others.

Born to Fly

To touch Great Spirit
You'll need to spread your wings and fly.

If you take a leap of faith
You will surely reach the sky.

We were born to fly.

Be Open

The Spirit of life
Flows freely
To and through
The souls
Who are open.

Be Cleansed

When you permit
The rivers of life
To flow over you
You will be cleansed
From the inside out.

Drink Spiritual Waters

Drink from many clean wells
And you will be nourished
By many waters.

Health Guidelines

Take control of what you can
And follow guidelines given
Focus on the positives
By them ensure you're driven.

Lessons Learnt

Today something has changed
I feel it deep within my soul
A shift has happened
There has been an
Awakening
Perhaps now
The virus can dissipate
Perhaps now – things will improve
Perhaps for now – lessons are learnt.

Held by the Vortex

The vortex within me
Spins wildly
It is the axis
That holds me
On the earth
And connects me
To the sky and its beings.
When she is ready
Mother Earth will
Release me
And I will shoot far
Into the void
That I call
Home.

A Kiss of Death

One sweet kiss
That's all it took
A stranger he was
But I knew he was mine – forever.

One sweet kiss
That's all it took
A stranger he was
But then I got sick – and was gone forever.

Take care & think twice – Covid

The Pendulum of Life

Without darkness there is no light
Without sadness there is no joy
Without others there is no love.

The pendulum of life
It swings back and forth
We can but prepare
For both ends of the spectrum.

Rain Fell

……and rain fell upon the earth
The people cried
For they understood not
That from the rain
Things blossom.

Water Love

Inside us all
Is a seed of love
That craves water to grow.

It's in the good
And in the bad
In us all – did you know?

For love
Does not separate
Nor choose where it will lay.

But we
All have a choice
To water love day by day.

Individual Drops

Each drop of the ocean
Remains individual
Whilst still being
Part of the whole.
Without the individual drops
There would be no ocean.

We are those drops.

Reaching Out

Always
Reach out
Don't Always be
Out of reach.

A Multi-Cultural Heart

I was born in the UK
I have lived in four countries
I have a Japanese name
White skin
Different coloured family
And a multi-cultural heart.

I am part of the whole
And represent the whole.

When I Look

When I look at you
I don't see your country
When I look at you
I don't see the colour of your skin.

When I look at you
I don't see rich or poor
When I look at you
I see your heart and soul
Another version of me.

One Heart, One Soul

Be not of hate
But of love
Be not jealous
But supportive
Be not judgement
But compassion.

The world needs spiritual people
From one heart
One mind
One soul.

Blossoms and Smiles

.....and for now dear friends
I will leave you in the hands of love
Where you can be moulded
Into the fullness of your beauty
Where you will blossom
And bring smiles
To many hearts and faces.

A Smile

One look
One smile
And suddenly
All heaviness was forgotten
The mind distracted with loving thoughts
The emotions busy with positive feelings
A reprieve from worries – given freely.

Without Words

We spoke deep into each other's hearts
Not one word was spoken
But all was understood.
A language without words
For those in touch with their true self.

Sing Your Song

Birds……
They sing from the depth of their soul
They worry not what others think
Their focus is purely on sharing
The song on their heart.

Never Alone

It's 3:14 am
Silence surrounds me
The heavens shine twinkling lights
Like energetic faces
Reminding us
We are never alone.

The Fog Lifts

...and the fog lifted
And the people realised
They weren't captives
They were free
To create
A new way
A new way of being.

Be Propelled

A shooting star
Is propelled forward
By the intensity
Of the force within it.

We too must be
Propelled forward
By the creative intensity
Within us.

Be Refreshed

It's time to turn the screen off
It's time to say goodnight
It's time to enter silence
It makes my heart feel light.

It's time to take some rest
And refresh my body and soul
It's time to nurture me
It keeps my spirit whole.

Find the Blessings

We have to find the blessing
In all things good and bad
It's easy when we're happy
But hard when we are sad.

But life has many lessons
That we all must take to heart
Sometimes it brings us closer
Sometimes it tears apart.

Angel of Death

……and their dead were gone
Like puffs of smoke
Up into the receiving sky.

Regrets were many
Tears fell like rain
And watered hope.

Hope grew
And they realised
There is no death….

Only a veil
Through to another existence.
Peace prevailed.

Life Goes On

The night unfolds
Darkness casts itself across the sky
Reaching the horizon.

Lights shine from streetlights
And from the cells of Covid prisoners
Everyone is on hold.

But life goes on, all around us
Look inwards for retrospection
But don't blind yourself to life.

Time to Sleep

The time has come to say goodnight
I know it's early – I wake with the light.

I'm often up at 3 am
If you're here, I'll see you then.

But just for now from screens I'll rest
Sweet dreams I pray and that you're blessed.

A Yarn to Be

The tumultuous seas are raging
Threatening to overwhelm
Anchor down, take control of thoughts
You're the captain at your helm.

Distract yourself with pleasures
Little things that keep you calm
This storm will pass on by
It will soon become a yarn.

Cradled In Peace

Darkness fills the sky
Not one light does shine
Not even from the heavens
Silence envelopes all.

Not even a whisper in the air
Everyone cradled in peace
I pray that same peace
Will fill your hearts always.

What a beautiful morning.

Be Love and Acceptance

A congruent heart doesn't offer love and acceptance
It **IS** love and acceptance.

Compassion

Compassion we need to be the difference
Compassion means acting through love
Then we will look and see the difference.
Acts of compassion are like angels above.

Be Kindness

Kindness….
It can be something you choose to show
Or something that you simply are.

True Happiness

Happiness can come from *things*
Happiness can come from *attitudes*
Happiness can come from *work*
But it is all temporary.

True inner happiness
Happens all on its own
It flows naturally
From the life giving waters of inner peace.

Isolation – An Opportunity

Self-isolation
Can be a great opportunity
To get to know yourself.

When you love and appreciate
Who you are alone with
It will be a pleasurable experience.

Isolation - an opportunity to grow.

Restrictions

Restrictions come
Like prison walls
Threatening to overwhelm.

Grasp the opportunities
Go within
You are at the helm.

Steer you boat
To greater depths
Than what you've known before.

Take this time
To look within
Reach your inner core.

Distraction

I sit
Quietly studying
Children
Outside
Making noise
I frown
Annoying
Contempt.

Into the Depths

Into the depths of tumultuous water
I tossed the hurt and pain
I freed myself of other's seeds
No longer giving them rain.

When all the seeds were gone and dead
New growth did start to sprout
Take a hold of all your pain
And throw it all right out.

Have No Regrets

Better we live our lives
Knowing we have disappointed another
Than we reach the end of life
Regretting that we have bitterly
Disappointed ourselves.

The Problem

The problem often is
That many spend their whole lives
Trying to not disappoint another
And whilst doing so
They inadvertently
Disappoint themselves.

Deafening Silence

Silence
To the spiritual hermit
Is pleasantly
Deafening

Perspectives

I know a boy
He stole my heart
Many years ago.

Such a joy
An infectious smile
Where did the time go?

Not many toys
No mobile phone
Just bush and natural play.

But still he found
That life was fun
Every single day.

Island Style

A shack to one
A palace to another
Beautiful people
All sisters and brothers.

Minimalist lives
Through circumstance not choice
Equal to all
And still have a voice.

Everyday
Whether they know you or not
They will smile
They don't care what you've got.

Cleansing Winds

The cleansing winds
Sweep through my mind
Carrying away
All that no longer serves me
Creating space
For growth and change.

Caught In a Web

I was caught in a web
I could feel the strands
Pressing back against my face.
I felt the panic and wondered
Would I ever escape?

Then suddenly I realised
The strands
Were just my fears.
They didn't have to imprison me
Not now or future years.

One by one
I broke the strands
All fear went away.
I found my inner freedom
Which I hold onto every day.

The Rainbow

The different colours
Gives it its uniqueness
It wouldn't be a rainbow
If it was all one colour.

Each colour just is
Each colour doesn't know it is different
It just forms part of the rainbow
We are the rainbow people.

Wake up and stop dreaming
Difference.

People of the Rainbow

We are all indigenous
To collective consciousness
Just as plants are indigenous
To the ground they grow in.

Their different colours
Are a normal occurrence
Of which we never question.

Collectively, different colours
Create the rainbow
As with people.

No Favourites

A round earth
Gently reminds us
That we all stand as equals
Upon her beautiful body.

Feet fixed firmly on the ground
We all have the same opportunity
To love and be loved
She holds no favourites.

No Hierarchy in Oneness

There is no hierarchy.
In collective consciousness
There is only
Individual aspects of consciousness
All equal, all necessary, all unique.

The world creates hierarchy
From fear of being nothing.

We Are One

We so often live our lives
Like fragmented parts
Never realising
That we are
One.

The Question to Ask

The question
To ask
Oneself
Daily
Is
Whether your relationship
With the whole
Is in fact whole.

The Sun Shines

The sun shines
At last
Like a lost love
Riding over the horizon
With eyes only for me
It pierces my entire being
Bringing fresh awareness to life.

Waiting

I'm waiting at the moment
Just waiting
I'm not sure what for
But I feel I need to wait.

In between waiting
And not waiting
Will be times of silence and stillness
In anticipation of the unknown.

The Edges of My Mind

Today I need to explore
The edges of my mind
I need to be extra
Self-loving and kind.

I need to have some space
To hear the inner voice
To find clear direction
Without all the noise.

I'll dip in and out today
I haven't completely gone
I'm still around loosely
And here for everyone.

Bringing Wholeness

The night draws in
The sun long gone
My pen is resting
Another chapter done.

Blood spilt and dried
Page after page
Shed many tears
But not any rage.

A book to inspire
To lift up the heart
Bringing wholeness
From fragmented parts.

Gender Neutral – The Key to Equality

When we see each person as a person
And not through gender
And recognise and accept
The male and female within ourselves
Equality can exist.

Gender issues - this is not a political issue
but a spiritual one.

Be the Change You Want to See

If you want change
Be that change
If you want love
Be love
In you want equality
Show equality.

The sun shines on all people.

True Power

True power is reflected from your spirit
Not the words shouted through your mouth.

True power is reflected in your gentle actions
They are the words that scream the loudest.

No one put a fire out with fire.

I Sneeze

I sneeze…….

Everyone scuttles
Like cockroaches
Thrust into light
Or when Tarantula
Suddenly appears.

Space…….
No longer cramped
Spare seat beside me
I smile to myself
It was only dust.

Stay Strong

Yesterday was a tough day
Muscle weakness took my strength
But not my spirit.

Stay strong in adversity
It won't last forever.

Heaven and Hell

Heaven and Hell
Defined by some as *'places'*
Defined by me as a *'state of being.'*

Micro Poetry

Book Four

Kenzo Amariyo

Gone but Not Forgotten

Gone but not forgotten
Carried in my heart
The veil of existence
And time keeps us apart.

But only in our body
Our spirits can still entwine
For love does not separate
In my heart your love will shine.

Sing

Sing
Sing from your heart
Like the sweet songs of the morn'
Sing your own song
Let it be as rivulets of joy
To all around you.

Flowing

I wish not to be soft or hard
Not to be up or down
But to be fluid
Flowing into all those unseen places
In your heart.

Silently

If you understand my silence
You will understand my words
The blood shed on my pages
Which may often sound absurd.

If you understand my silence
You'll know silently I'm here
Silence hasn't forgotten
I quietly feel your tears.

River of Compassion

She sat and wept
Not for herself
For humanity.

Her tears fell
Like angelic dewdrops
Watering the earth.

From her tears
Grew a tree of love
That stood by a river of compassion.

Success is In the Climb

I'm successful
Without a best seller
I'm successful
Because I put pen to paper
I wrote that which was on my heart
And completed it.

Anything else is a bonus.

Perceptions

Water reflects
That which we think we see
Perceptions
May be different
For you and for me.

New Buds

Spring is on its way
New buds
New life
Breaking the chrysalis
I fly.

Green Fingers

One flower
Many seeds
Plant wisely
Harvest the good crops
Turn over the bad crops
If you ignore them
They will still grow.

I Just Know

I don't have to see you
Or hear you speak
I know when you're good
And when you feel weak.

I live by my senses
They speak to my soul
They tell me the truth
And if you feel whole.

Don't say you're great
When you're down as you do
I know the truth
Way before you.

Listen to the Call

The mountains call
I hear the song
I lift up my head
It won't be long.

Connect Daily

Feel her rhythm
Hear her beat
Mother earth
Beneath your feet.

Take off your shoes
And close your eyes
Don't miss this chance
It may go by.

Breathe her in
She'll heal your heart
And cleanse your mind
A brand new start.

Slay that Giant

Touch the pain you feel inside
Be conscious of it, don't let it hide.

Giants are often hard to slay
Give it your all, and maybe pray.

The universe is on your side
Slay that giant, stand with pride.

Face your pain everyday
Be its master, have your say.

Clouds Hang Low

Clouds hang low
From a hidden blue sky
The view is obscured
But it is still there.

Likewise:

Clouds can hang low
From the hidden blue sky of our minds
Dreams become obscured
But they are still there.

Look past the clouds.

Stand Tall

Together we all stand tall
We all stand strong
To believe in something different
Doesn't make you wrong.

Reach out to those around you
Lift them past clouds above
We all stand as equals
So please share all your love.

Accepting Now

Feeling down or discouraged
Often comes from a misunderstanding
Between where you are in a situation
And where you think you should be.

Acceptance of the *'now'* is the key to moving forward.

Experiences

Experiences can shape us or break us
It all depends
Upon what you do with it.

Reflections

He who holds beauty in his heart
Reflects beauty onto all things
He who holds love in his heart
Reflects love onto all things.

Be the reflection the world needs.

Words

Words can paint a thousand pictures
They tell me everything I want to hear
But actions paint the deeper truths
They paint your spirit loud and clear.

Love

Love to the heart
Is like nectar
To the bee.

Reality

Who decides that reality is really reality?
Perhaps that which we think of as dreams
Is our true reality
Perhaps that which we think of as reality
Is really a dream
Maybe we are living a dream
And need to find our reality!

Wake Up, Wake Up Everyone

In the early hours of day
Many sleeping the night away
I sat quite still, an owl I heard
I understood, quite absurd.

He said that much of life goes by
When sleeping late with heavy eye
It stops us greeting our dear sun
Wake up, wake up, everyone.

Count Your Blessings

Count your blessings every day
Look for the good, mind what you say
Be kind to others, forgive the hurt
Catch yourself, don't be curt
Everyone carries pain of their own
Everyone reaps, what they have sown.

Sadness

Sadness covers the weary soul
With smudged windows don't you know?
Things loved become shallow pools
You feel down cast, such a fool.

Clean your windows raise your head
Stand tall, you are not dead
Let the beauty all around
Lift your spirit from the ground.

Inner Peace

Gaining inner peace is easy
But holding onto it in turbulent seas
Is a real test of fortitude.

Success

Some fight their way to the top
Others crawl their way to the top.
I'm riding on the wings of Spirit
And it may or may not be to the top.

Success happens on the inside.

Spiritual Enlightenment

It is not by power
Nor by might
That we conquer the world
But by the fruits of spiritual
enlightenment.

Softly, Softly

Softly, softly
She treads bare foot
Through the depth of the wood
Feet caressing the mossy earth
Flesh to flesh two worlds meet
Hers and the universe.

Silence Within

Silence within
Brimming over
With the fullness of life
Quiet whispers
In my soul
Gifts my heart with wings.

What Is Life?

What is life if it isn't about sharing love
Offering compassion
And being the best version of you?

The Curtains are Drawn

It's the end of the day….
Darkness has closed its curtains
In order for someone else to have light.

And tomorrow they will open again
Like a grand opening
For an exquisite opera.

Find Your Centre

Rush, rush, rush
Like a tumultuous river
Not knowing where it is going
Just going
Pushed by yesterday
And in amongst it all
A rock……
Stillness is its name
Unmoved by the river.

Riches

I remember sitting on the wall at Westward Ho
Legs swinging, breeze blowing
Sun shining, sea lapping onto the golden sand
Smiles, laughter, seagulls squawking.

It's funny how simple things bring so much pleasure.
Riches – measured by the moments we embrace.

Catalyst for Change

We can complain about our situation
Or circumstances as much as we like.
But if we want something to change,
We must be the catalyst for that change.

Mindfulness

Mindfulness
The ability to be quietly conscious
Of all that is
Whilst remaining centred and unmoved.

Silence

Silence
No thoughts
Just awareness
Awareness of the
Stillness within
At peace.

Sunset

The sun kisses the horizon
Peace falls all around
Birds still sing
Another day gone
Dusk.

Functional Neurological Disorder

FND is not my FrieND
Sometimes it sends me round the bend
Twitches, jerks, chronic pain
Crawly feelings again and again.

Can't run, jump, dance or walk
But I'll not be beat, I walk my talk
Life still is good, I'm not here whining
For every cloud has a silver lining.

Dementia

She slaps
She spits
Pulls at your hair
Her nails dig your skin
She doesn't care.

Or so you think
Now look really deep
You'll feel her pain
It will make you weep.

She's tired, she's lonely
Confused, with great fear
So please be kind
Your day may be near.

The Pains of Dementia

I look through my windows
See those who I love
Standing before me
Gifts from above.

I see them smiling
Talking to me
But I don't understand
In different worlds are we.

I try to reach out
But nothing will move
Trapped, isolated
Needle not in the groove.

How Beautiful Life Is

And there it was……
She flung open the window of her mind
And saw just how beautiful life is.

Sparkling Dew

Sparkling dew, threads of silk
Grass now covered in natures milk.

Leaves now gone and trees stand bare
Look around, gifts everywhere.

What we have in this short life
Often brings a lot of strife.

Take the time, appreciate the earth
Breathe in deeply, a second birth.

It's Not about You

There are times
When you just have to accept
That no matter how much patience you have
How much love you offer
How much you give
How much you try
For some people
It will never be enough.

In such times
You must remember
It's not about you
It is their issue, not your own.

Every Time

Every time she speaks hurtful words
I remind myself
That she cuts me to pieces
Because she has been cut to pieces
And needs someone to feel her pain.

It doesn't lessen the effect it has
But it removes all temptations for
revenge.

Toxic Relationships

There comes a time
When you just have to end
Toxic relationships
Even if he/she is family.

The cost of keeping them going
Can be too great
Free yourself
You can't change them.

But you can decide
Whether they should still be in your life.
Sometimes
We just have to let go.

Prepare

Prepare your mind and your heart
To receive the best that life has to offer.

Then when it comes
You will be ready to receive.

Prepare the ground
Before you plant the seed
Not afterwards.

Don't Limit Yourself

Never limit your view of self or life based on your past.
Your past is your past.
It doesn't have to inform your future.

Your Smile Shines

Just as the moon shines brightly
So too does your smile shine
It lights up my life and heart
It touches places others can't
It is a priceless gift
That only you can give.

Other Titles by the Author

The Effects of Shamanic Healing & Other Healing Practices on Well-Being

Poems for Loved Ones – In Remembrance of All Those Who Have Returned Home

Spiritual Healing – A Guide to Getting Started

Poems for Christians – In Christ We Live - In Christ We Die

True Ghost Stories – Working with the Other Side

Poems of Childhood Pain – The Effect of Sexual Abuse on Children

Urinalysis, Alkalinity & Well-Being